FINS & THE FIFTIES

MIKE KEY

TONY THACKER

FINS & THE FIFTIES

MIKE KEY

TONY THACKER

OSPREY

Published in 1987 by Osprey Publishing Limited
27A Floral Street, London WC2E 9DP
Member company of the George Philip Group

British Library Cataloguing in Publication Data

Key, Mike
    Fins & the fifties.
    1. Automobiles—History
    I. Title   II. Thacker, Tony
    629.2'222'09045   TL15
ISBN 0-85045-810-2

Design Matthew Evans

Filmset by Tameside Filmsetting Limited,
Ashton-under-Lyne, Lancashire
Printed in Hong Kong

Endpapers **Future Buick looking a lot like a Cadillac with that tail-light and rear-wing treatment and those projectiles. Wildcat show car became the '54 Skylark**

Page 2/3 **Chrysler's DeSoto division had one of its best years in 1957. This is the Firedome Sportsman for which twin antennas and dual headlamps were optional**

CONTENTS

Acknowledgements	**7**
Introduction	**9**
At least the 1948 show	**13**
Lead sleds and the bucktooth Buick	**25**
Firepower	**35**
Buy me and stop one	**43**
All aboard the Skylark	**51**
The shape of fins to come	**61**
The hot one	**71**
Get your kicks on Route 66	**83**
On the road and all shook up	**97**
At the hop	**113**
More Americans have more	**123**

ACKNOWLEDGEMENTS

When we conceived this book it was going to be a simple, colourful tribute to the cars of the fifties. Somewhere along the way we took a turning which led us to publish something infinitely more complicated but satisfyingly more interesting. Therefore a lot of material that Mike photographed was dropped in favour of original advertising brochures which exactly illustrate the flavour of fifties styling. As our ideas expanded to produce more than just another car book, so we went in search of other contemporary material to illustrate that exciting period. Our search led us to sources as diverse as McDonald's and *Playboy* magazine, and thankfully everybody was enthusiastic and helpful. We would therefore like to thank all

Ford's attempt at an American sports car appeared late in the summer of 1954 and was relatively unchanged for 1955. It did, however, receive a larger, 292 ci, V8 engine

those listed below, without whose help this book could not have been produced:

Colin Burnham (**pp. 22–23, 76–77, 110–111, 115**); *CC* magazine (**pp. 6, 109**); Pat Ganahl (**pp. 14, 16, 30, 114**); John Hillelson Agency Ltd (**pp. 126–127**); Warren Hokinson (**p. 16**); *Hot Rod* magazine (**p. 17**); Jim Jacobs (**pp. 28, 38**); Paul Kunkel (**pp. 17, 36, 52, 54, 104**); David Loehr (**p. 73**); London Features International Ltd (**pp. 72, 105**); McDonald's Corporation (**p. 88**); National Motor Museum (**endpapers, pp. 24, 29, 37, 48–49, 53, 59–60, 63, 64–65, 67, 84–85, 86–87, 92–93, 98–99, 100–101, 106–107, 114, 116–117, 118–119, 124, 128**); Petrified Film Incorporated (**pp. 42, 82, 120–121**); Pictorial Press (**p. 46**); *Playboy* magazine (**p. 57**); Estate of Elvis Presley (**p. 89**); Barry Wheeler (**pp. 46, 88**).

INTRODUCTION

You might be wondering what gives us the right to compile this book. Well, we were both born in the late forties, Mike in 1946 and myself just one month before the calendar was thrown away for a new decade. Though born into the extremely grey world of post-war Britain, we were fifties kids colouring our lives with the sounds of America. We couldn't drive—we were much too young—and besides, petrol was rationed, hardly anybody was driving in England. But in America Chuck Berry was chasing Maybellene's Coupe DeVille in his V8 Ford and for us that was more or less where it started and stopped.

Dodge, along with most other manufacturers, restyled for 1955, adding twin tail-lights topped by a chrome fin

Strangely, neither of us owns a fifties car, but both our garages contain a pair of V8 Fords and Mike's is also home for a '40 Chevy sedan and a '40 Plymouth coupé and that's enough to be going on with.

We both have a strange nostalgia for those uncomplicated days when we formed our affiliations with rock 'n' roll and Detroit, and in our opinion that gives us as much right as anybody to write this book. Besides, we have both been photographing and writing about cars for far longer than we care to remember. We hope you enjoy it.

Tony Thacker & Mike Key
England, 1987

AT LEAST THE 1948 SHOW

The war ended in 1945 with a huge sigh of relief, heard loudly in Detroit where at last it was back to business as usual. And the business was, in the words of Henry Ford, 'Building motors and putting them on wheels'. During the war years Detroit, like all manufacturing centres, had been busy with armaments, and automobile design had hardly moved forward since 1939. Technology had, however, progressed dramatically, as it usually does in the face of adversity, and Detroit readied itself for the new age—an age of prosperity when the automobile would no longer be only a mere means of transport. Instead it would be the time machine to Utopia; a world of soaring futuristic space-age cities held up as the backdrop for the truly modern automobile.

For Detroit the future could not be conceived until at least the 1948 show because that would be the earliest that they could get anything other than face-lifted pre-war designs into production. They were not alone in their concepts

Left **Though physically unchanged from '46, Pontiac for '48 introduced a new three-bar grille dubbed triple 'Silver Streaks'; it was still topped by their famous 'tin Indian'**

Previous page **Buick bared its teeth in 1949 and designer Ned Nickles introduced us to Ventiports through which, using a Ventiport key, the hood was opened**

though, because all over America there were guys cutting the hell out of their cars in order to update them and try to recapture the lost excitement of conflict.

People began modifying their carriages from the moment they made them horseless—the war was merely a disastrous hiccup in the development programme. Once over, it was back to the garage and on with the search for speed.

Auto racing in the USA was almost exclusively confined to short oval circuits, more often than not horse-racing tracks or banked wooden autodromes. The ultimate was the Indianapolis Motor Speedway, the Brickyard, which had opened in 1909. North America's only other motor racing mecca was Daytona Beach, Florida, where there had been speed trials, including land speed record attempts, and a board speedway for many years. There had not actually been a road race in America since 1934 and what racing there was certainly was not organized on a national scale, and in

California it was hardly organized at all.

Come the weekend, guys would drive their stripped-down Ford hot rods to the dry lakes of the Mojave Desert and in the cool dawn race *en masse* across the lake beds. Only those out in front, and therefore the fastest, could see, the also-rans being clouded in kicked-up alkali dust. The ensuing mêlée caused many accidents, as did late-night sorties, soon attracting the attention of the authorities. It was organize or the end, and that was no alternative. So in 1937 the lakes racers organized themselves into the Southern California Timing Association and kept a low profile until Muroc, the most popular venue, was closed in 1940 to become Edwards Air Force Base. It would never again be used for time trials but there were plenty of other venues, including the street.

Street racing was strictly illegal but there were a lot of guys who could not be bothered with the 100-mile drive out to the desert. Stop-light racing was nearer home and, what's more, the track was open every day. All one had to do was keep one eye open for the cops and the other on the light.

The cops were always around though, and pretty soon it was that familiar story: get organized or get busted. The

Above **New for '49, Lincoln shared many body pressings with sister Mercury; however, the grille was different and the Lincoln had sunken headlights which customizers emulated**

Top left **Rodding was always fun in an early Ford but to begin with the modifications were minimal: a pair of duals, some whitewalls and a couple of kids**

Centre left **Rodders liked to cruise their cars covered in lakes dust, but their actions were destroying the lakes.**
Picture courtesy of the Pat Ganahl Collection

Bottom left **Two Model A Ford hot rods drag racing through the streets of Los Angeles in the early forties.**
Picture courtesy of the Pat Ganahl Collection

smart ones got organized and the first legal drag race was held late in 1948 on a back road of the Santa Barbara airport in Goleta, California, under the auspices of the Santa Barbara Acceleration Association. Disused roads and redundant airfields all over America were soon being quickly converted into dragstrips.

The rapid growth of the sport saw the further development of those dry-lakes racing hot rods—almost exclusively late-twenties and early-thirties Fords with hopped-up original engines or transplanted V8s from later Fords and Mercurys. They were cheap, fast and fun.

Unfortunately, the rodders were rapidly destroying the dry lakes with their irresponsible charges and a new venue for flat-out fun was desperately sought. Three representatives of the hot rod fraternity, Pete Petersen, Lee Ryan and Wally Parks, journeyed up to Utah and obtained an agreement to hold the annual Bonneville Nationals on the Great Salt Lake. The event still takes place but the top speed recorded at that first meeting was an amazing 185 mph.

Driving right alongside the hot rodders were another bunch of enthusiasts who, though they had the same dusty dry-lakes roots, were concerned more with appearance than speed. They modified their cars to look sharp rather than go fast, and they also took their turning on to the road to fame in 1948 when the first hot rod car show was held at the Los Angeles National Guard Armory.

The show was a huge success, as was a new magazine launched at the show. *Hot Rod* magazine was the brain-wave of Robert E. 'Pete' Petersen and Bob Lindsay, and the first print-run of 10,000 copies was a sell-out at the show. The magazine immediately went monthly from that first January issue and, looking back, the boys had no trouble filling its pages. It seemed like the whole country was car

HOT ROD OF THE MONTH
Sitting in the driver's seat is Eddie Hulse, who, a few moments after this picture was taken, drove number 668, to set a new SCTA record for Class C roadsters. Hulse, a native Californian, nosed out Randy Shinn, a long-time top honor holder for the RC Class. Shinn's old record was 129.40 in a channeled Mercury T.

Above **The post-war years were grey, well, black and white, as was the first issue of Pete Petersen's *Hot Rod* magazine of January 1949, but it was a sell-out anyway**

Top left **Oval track racing at Saugus, California, in 1947 with Stan Cross (87) and Mickey Cory going the wrong way.**
Picture courtesy of Warren Hokinson

Bottom left **Long-nosed straight-six or eight powered '32 Ford roadster kicking dust at the dry lakes in the forties.**
Picture courtesy of the Pat Ganahl Collection

crazy. On the East Coast they were going round in circles (they still are) because in 1948 Bill France organized the Daytona Beach boys and the Southern circle trackers into the National Association for Stock Car Auto Racing.

A hopped-up pre-war jalopy was not everybody's idea of a stylish ride and the more discerning driver sought something more up to date, though none the less individual.

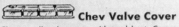

18

As we have seen, Detroit was understandably a little slow in providing the public the transport it desired. The alternative was to take something outdated and customize it.

This new word was coined to describe alterations which ranged from the popular substitution of a new chrome grille insert, an easy updating addition, continental spare-wheel kit and almost mandatory dual exhausts to full-blown body mods including, possibly, a roof chop and a lacquer paint job. Fords were still the most popular for modifying but Chevys, Buicks and Plymouths, in fact anything, were suitable fodder for the customizer.

Fitting chrome doo-dads was an easy do-it-yourself job, but to handle the more extreme mods a new type of body shop emerged, the epitome of which was that operated by the Barris brothers. George Barris had driven down to Los Angeles from Sacramento in a radical '36 Ford having learned his trade under the legendary customizer Harry Westergard. George was joined by his brother Sam and they put the 'K' in kustomizing when they opened Barris Kustom Autos in Lynwood, California, in 1945. Pretty soon they became involved with the movie set. Sam was hot stuff at metalwork but George excelled in promotion—self-promotion—and was soon advising and appearing in films, writing and photographing technical features for the first generation of custom car magazines as well as selling his art and ideas to anybody who would buy them. George rapidly became 'King of the Kustomizers'.

Left **Continental kits, alternative grilles and various chrome doo-dads for dressing up both the inside and outside of the car were popular accessories then and now**

Right **The mandatory modification was the addition of dual pipes, either fake or for real. Some improved performance and some just sounded like they did. The fakes did nothing**

Above **When the rodders came in from the lakes they were herded together at the Los Angeles National Guard Armory for all to see—the hot rod show had come to town**

Right **Body shops specializing in customizing emerged in the late forties and chopped tops, louvres, sunken headlights and different grilles were the order of the day**

Nobody knows for sure how much effect these street trends had on the cars being produced by the major manufacturers. Some would say that all their influences came from Europe, but these were American designers working on American cars with American influences and it was impossible for them to ignore the revolution going on around them. Certainly, the origins may have been European, but what was to evolve over the next decade was pure American affluence.

The first significant post-war development came from Hudson in the form of unitary construction, 'with famous "Step-Down" design' and a choice of L-head six- or eight-cylinder engines. The latter in 'Super Eight' series produced 121 bhp from its 262 cubic inches and a good power base for its forthcoming career on Southern stock car circuits.

The Hudson also had independent front suspension but then so did the new Lincolns. Henry Ford's grandson Benson had taken control of the Lincoln-Mercury division, the two marques sharing many body pressings, and their new offering for 1949, introduced on 22 April 1948, was the Cosmopolitan. Except for sunken headlights and more chrome it looked pretty much like the Mercury announced a week later. At $1000 less, it is no wonder that the Merc outsold the Lincoln many times over. Besides, its price and easily-tuned Ford-based flathead V8 soon endeared it to the customizers.

Both Buick and their buyers were content with the '46 model, which looked an awful lot like the '41 model; however, it had a lot more cohesive style than its contemporaries. Nevertheless, they courted the modern motorist with 'Dynaflow', Detroitese for torque converter transmission.

The following year Buick bared bigger teeth while stylist Ned Nickles introduced us to the luxury of Ventiports. Portholes to you and me, and there they hung on the side, useless, until they fell off in 1958.

While one division of the General's army played at styling, another, Cadillac, advanced the technical boundary by announcing a compact 331 ci ohv V8 producing 160 bhp. The bodies were largely unaltered from the previous pressings but they did introduce an industry first: the pillarless, two-door convertible Coupe DeVille which so inspired Chuck Berry. What Cadillac really had to shout

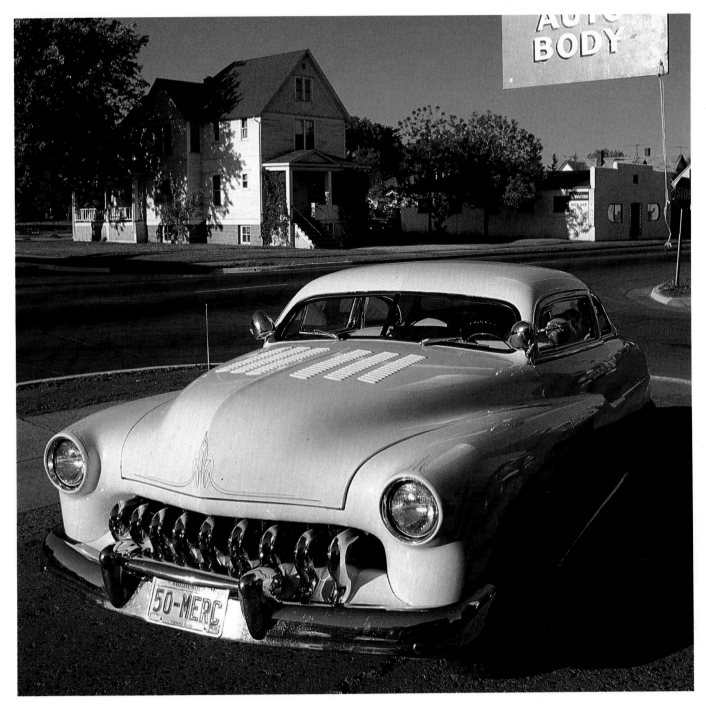

about was that new engine—and people heard all right and soon were replacing their old side-valve Fords with Caddy's ohv, creating a generation of Fordillacs.

Oldsmobile also débuted an ohv V8 in 1949. Tagged the Rocket V8, they slotted it into their lightweight '48 Futuramic model, called it the Eighty-Eight and in so doing built the first factory hot rod. They cleaned up too, 'Red'

Byron becoming NASCAR champion after Olds won six of that year's nine NASCAR events.

Hudson also had a good year in 1949, their best in fact; production exceeded 140,000 units, profits were over $10 million, and the new 112 bhp six-cylinder Pacemaker kept them out in front at the ovals. Sadly, they would not be able to sustain this success far into the fifties.

LEAD SLEDS AND THE BUCKTOOTH BUICK

1950

If Buick had bared its teeth in 1949, it was only a prelude to the full-frontal attack launched in 1950. Many have said they went too far with the 'bucktooth Buick' which had appeared midway through the previous year in a new 1950 Special line. But who are we to argue with the public who bought Buicks by the bucketful, half a million of them, pushing Buick up to third place in the sales race behind Chevrolet and Ford. Buick symbolized success both for itself and for the buyers of its automobiles. Elsewhere in the world, Russia too showed its teeth when it announced it possessed an atomic bomb.

Success was also in sight for Cadillac at the unlikely venue of Le Mans, France, where a Caddy-powered Allard came third. Two others also placed in the race: an almost stock Series 62 coupé was tenth and a special-bodied Series 62 was 11th. Surprising results considering their ever-increasing size and shape—as slab-sided as New York's UN building, dismissed at the time as 'a great idea gone wrong'.

Left **Buick's teeth grew even bigger for 1950, earning them the nickname 'bucktooth'—some said they went too far. There were three models: Super, Special and Roadmaster**

Previous page **Bob Hirohata's Merc was the most famous built by the Barris brothers. The original is hidden away in LA; this is a faithful replica built by Jack Walker**

25

Chevrolet had little to offer in 1950 that had not been available the previous year and all their ad men could write about was a fully-automatic Powerglide transmission and a two-door hardtop called the Bel Air. They could hardly be heard, though, over the shouts of Senator Joseph McCarthy who was colour-blind to everything except red.

Mercury could not match Chevy's 1½ million sales but they did make their millionth automobile that year. What changes they made were small, but a significant addition to the range was the Monterey coupé which featured a padded canvas or vinyl top and a custom leather interior. Ford tried similar treatment on its special-edition Crestliner and in so doing won the coveted Fashion Academy Award for the second year.

The influences of the street trends were certainly being felt and the '49 to '51 Merc was, and always will be, one of

Above **Ford offered '50 improvements for '50', but basically they were the '49ers. This is a Custom DeLuxe Club coupé but customers have always been happy to create their own**

Left **Chevy's line for '50 was also basically their 1949 models with new grilles and trim changes. The Fleetline Special, seen here, had sweeping modern fastback styling but essentially the 1937 'Stovebolt' six engine. Nevertheless, sales reached a record 1.5 million**

the customizer's favourite cars. The Barris brothers were undoubtedly responsible for its impact by chopping and channelling a '51 for owner Bob Hirohata. Other features incorporated into his car included full fender skirts with 1950 Cadillac-style fake air scoops, a floating single-bar grille to replace the stock shiny coil type, sunken headlights à la '49 Lincoln, frenched '52 Lincoln tail-lights and

Buick 'Sweapspear' side-trim. It set a trend which has been repeated on custom cars ever since and the Hirohata Merc, as it has always been known, is still around.

The idea of custom car shows was really beginning to catch on and the first Annual National Roadster Show was held in Oakland, California, on 19 January. The event still takes place and its accolade for America's Most Beautiful Roadster remains the most coveted. The winner that year was Bill Niekamp with his track-style roadster built on an Essex chassis with parts from four Model A Ford bodies and a 1942 Mercury engine. The car survives, having been restored by its present owner, Jim Jacobs.

Another milestone event was also taking place in

Above **A baby Hudson was Hudson's new baby for 1950. It looked low and featured a new horizontal four-bar grille, and it cleaned up on the NASCAR stock car circuits**

Top left **To compete with GM and Chrysler two-door hardtops, Mercury introduced their Monterey coupé which has long been a favourite of the customizers**

Bottom left **Winner of the first Annual National Roadster Show and the title 'America's Most Beautiful Roadster' was Bill Niekamp with his track-style, Merc-motored roadster**

California when, on 19 June, C. J. 'Pappy' Hart opened the world's first commercial dragstrip at what was the Orange County airport in Santa Ana. Prior to this Pappy and his friends had raced, up to eight abreast—that way, hardly

29

anybody lost!—at Mile Square, but they were eventually kicked off the US Navy property by the Marines.

To begin with the competitors at Santa Ana were mostly driving stockers but gradually the dry lakesters stopped playing in the sand, got used to a short, smooth sprint, and the sport of serious drag racing had started. Meanwhile, up at Bonneville Dean Batchelor and Alex Xydias put an end to the misconception that hot rods were incapable of exceeding 200 mph by breaking an old Auto Union record. With a single Ford flathead engine in their So-Cal Special they turned 210 mph. The battle for the record books had begun.

Above **Pontiac Chieftain Super DeLuxe Catalina two-door hardtop coupé. Paint schemes for 1950 were San Pedro Ivory, Sierra Rust or two-tone combinations of the two**

Top left **Rodders raced anything and everything including aeroplane fuel tanks, but the Hernandez & Meeks roadster, seen here at El Mirage in the early fifties, ran 149 mph**

Bottom left **Two roadsters get ready for the off at an SCTA organized drag race at the Blimp Base in El Toro near Santa Ana. Pictures courtesy of the Pat Ganahl Collection**

Unfortunately, another battle zone had also opened up, this time in Korea. Meanwhile, in Britain petrol rationing had ended—now all that was needed to go places were cars.

1951
FIREPOWER

In automotive terms 1951 could almost be dismissed because not a whole lot happened. Cinema audiences, however, were discovering Marlon Brando, who was happening, in his third film, *A Streetcar Named Desire*. They were also watching Bogey and Hepburn in *The African Queen* which, good though it was, was nothing compared to the gritty, stark realism of Brando's street acting. In England a down-to-earth, almost back-to-the-earth, radio serial, which is still broadcast today, began: it was called *The Archers*.

It was all quiet on the Western front—well, as far west as Detroit, where Ford were offering the latest version of their '49 model, a new Custom DeLuxe Victoria two-door hardtop. Popular though these Fords might have been, the design was half-baked, or at least the scale model was, in the kitchen oven of designer Dick Caleal. Ford also introduced the first fully-automatic Ford-O-Matic transmission but the engine was basically the same old side-valve design

Left **There was always plenty of speed equipment available for the Ford flathead, including these Ardun ohv conversions, but with the arrival of Chrysler's hemi its days were numbered**

Previous page **Chevrolet created a wider look for '51 by moving the parking lamps into the lower grille—custom version takes it further with chopped top and shaved hood**

HOP UP

AUG 1951

15¢

- HOT RODS
- CUSTOMS
- MOTORCYCLES
- RACING
- BOATS

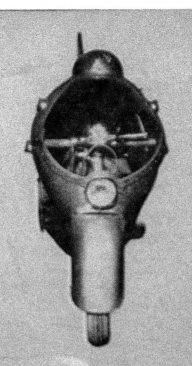

Performance Unlimited!

NEW HUDSON HORNET

Introducing the H-145 Engine with Miracle H-Power

introduced in 1932.

Until now that engine had been Ford's strength because, despite GM's various ohv V8s, there was 20 years' experience with the side-valve plus an abundance of aftermarket speed equipment which made it the racers' favourite. There was even an Ardun ohv conversion which had been designed for dustcart installation in England, but the flattie was about to become redundant because Chrysler announced its 331 ci hemi-head Firepower V8 for their top-of-the-line New Yorker. It produced an unheard-of 180 bhp and was, at the time, America's most powerful car.

Oldsmobile were still doing well at the track where they won almost half of the NASCAR Grand National events and

Above **The new Hornet was really a Commodore with a high-performance six and rocketship-shaped 'Badges of Power' on the side mouldings—it did well and set new NASCAR record**

Left Hop Up **was the latest customizing magazine to hit the news-stands. It was popular because of its small format: it could easily be hidden inside a school book**

easily took the championship title. Their reign too was almost over, though.

On the street 1951 saw the publication of another magazine aimed at hot rodders and customizers. *Hop Up*, which was pocket-sized and could be easily hidden inside a school book, appeared in September and had George Barris as one of its main contributors providing 'Custom Hints'.

Chevys were already showing their metal and the following year a young GM car stylist called Harry Bradley would purchase a '51 and turn it into another famous custom car, La Jolla. Harry, now a lecturer at the Art Center of California, still drives the car.

At the drags there were two significant events: the National Hot Rod Association, drag racing's governing body, was formed under the leadership, then and now, of Wally Parks. The other new arrival was that of the first real rail job, the term describing a race car consisting of hardly more than an engine and a pair of chassis rails. The car in question was an old lakes racer campaigned since the thirties but lengthened and fitted with a variety of engines by new

Above **For 1951 Ford made only detail changes to the grille, tail-lights and interior but they also introduced the Victoria. This, however, is the two-door sedan**

Top left **In the early days there was no definition between cars built for go and cars built for show. This is Bill Niekamp in AMBR at El Mirage about to run 142 mph**

Bottom left **Mercury redesigned its grille and tail-lights for 1951 and did well on the NASCAR circuits, but the era of this classic shape was about to end**

owner LeRoy Neumayer. Fundamentally, No. 25 set the style for all future dragsters and it is still owned by Art Chrisman who was given the car when LeRoy joined the army.

BUY ME AND STOP ONE

Though nothing significant happened to their model range for 1952, Chevrolet understood that they had to do something. Sure, they had market leadership but that was not enough, the cars were dull. With the appointment of chief engineer Ed Cole, Chevy began to transform their product line, with Cole actively supporting Harley Earl's idea for a sports roadster.

Chevy's potential for the future may have been set at the second Annual Oakland Roadster Show, when Joe Bailon took first place in the custom category with his '41 coupé and Spence Murray took second with his chopped '49 two-door. Third place went to a somewhat sick George Barris who had no less than seven entries. Murray, who worked for *Hop Up*, later took the Chevy on a 5000-mile trip to Indianapolis, generating on the way massive interest in the Californian cult of customizing.

The racing bug was also spreading as new dragstrips opened up all over America. Los Angeles gained a

Left **Next year's models now—this GM stylist shows us what to expect from Chevrolet, America's number one manufacturer, the following year . . .**

Previous page . . . **basically a new grille which featured Chevrolet's first teeth. Korean war caused a materials shortage and finish, particularly of chrome, was poor**

43

44

permanent strip which is still in use at the County Fairgrounds in Pomona.

Though it sometimes seems that Americans can only race in straight lines or circles, that theory was disproved in 1952 when Lincoln-Mercury went racing. They had expected to have the new ohv V8 that year to power their new model, which was rather ugly when compared to the classic '49 to '51 cars, but it wasn't ready in time. Nevertheless, veteran mechanic Bill Stroppe persuaded Lincoln to give him cars for the Carrera Panamericana, known simply as the Mexican road race, and he repayed them by taking first to fourth in his class. Winner Chuck Stevenson finished almost one hour

Above and left **On the street anything and everything was available, from fender skirts for those cars that didn't come with them to reversible hide seat covers. There was some confusion, though, as to whether to add some chrome or to take it off. Traditional customizers took it off; those who didn't know added it, and everything else, on**

ahead of the 1951-winning Ferrari.

Lincoln, taking advantage of their new-found performance image, restyled their range for 1952, added a two-door hardtop sports coupé, the Capri, to the line-up and announced a new division, headed by William Clay Ford, to handle the soon-to-be-reintroduced Continental.

Buick were, despite acres of chrome, suffering from a lack of lustre. In the end they would go totally over the top, but for the time being they made do with America's first four-barrel carburettor, now the industry standard.

Something else went into production that year which we grew to rely upon almost as much as the four-barrel carb: the contraceptive pill. In England, the nation lost both its King, George VI, and its identity—ID cards were taken away. But the country had the atom bomb which was tested in the Monte Bello Islands, I've looked for them on the map but I can't find them. However, I found Agatha Christie's *The Mousetrap* which opened in London's West End in 1952 and is still running. Different cast, though.

Above **DeLuxe Chevys were distinguished by extra chrome mouldings everywhere, including the merest hint of the shape of fins to come atop the rear wing**

Top left **The West was busy experimenting with the big bang. The British sensibly chose to experiment far from home; the Americans blew up their own backyard—Nevada**

Bottom left **The inspiration for America's automotive stylists came out of the air, in this case the DeHavilland 110 Sea Vixen showing its own brand of power**

In South America Eva Peron died, while in North America General Dwight D. Eisenhower ascended to the presidency. Also in its ascendency was the DeHavilland 110 jet fighter which broke the sound barrier that year.

ALL ABOARD THE SKYLARK

The significance of the jet age and supersonic flight was not lost on GM's chief stylist Harley Earl, who is reported to have visited an airbase and seen in the tail fins the future for automotive styling. Whether that is true or not does not matter; the influence manifested itself one way or another on almost every American automobile—even Hudson, whose image and sales were plummeting like an out-of-control plane. This year they would lose, rather than make, $10 million, and in an effort to recapture their lost youth market they offered 'Twin H-power' and a 7-X racing engine for 'severe usage', and christened the new model Super Jet but adorned it with a fake air scoop. Nevertheless, they won

more than half the NASCAR events and their driver Herb Thomas took the championship title.

People had gone power crazy; more than half Dodge's

Top left **Despite competition from the ohvs, Ford continued to be 'the car' to have if you were a performance enthusiast—more than half of the production were V8s**

Bottom left **Chevy lost two teeth that year but plugged the gap with chrome-rimmed parking lamps. The one-piece windscreen was also new for 1953**

Previous page **Harley Earl's Corvette, though owing little to contemporary styling, was stunning. In Polo White only, Chevrolet managed to sell just 300**

HONK!

CUSTOM CARS • HOT RODS

WHY a HOT IGNITION?
By Ak Miller

MAY 1953
25c

• SPARKLING CUSTOMS • UNIQUE HOT RODS
• MECHANICAL and CONSTRUCTION DETAILS

As colorful as the autumn

MULTI-COLOR PLAID with BOLTA-QUILT one-and-one-quarter-inch channel bolster, trimmed with vinyl leatherette and rayon.

BLUE STRIPE PLASTIC—Blue moire leatherette and rayon trim.

customers chose the new Red Ram hemi-head 241 ci V8. To prove its worth, Dodge took a '54 model to Bonneville and set 196 new records. It also topped all other V8s in the Mobilgas Economy Run.

Late in the year Dodge displayed a futuristic sports roadster called the Firearrow. It ran but it would not go into production, unlike Harley Earl's idea for Chevrolet, the Corvette. This was one of the few Motorama dream cars, being based on the 1952 EX-122 show car, that would go into production virtually unchanged.

Though small and simple by American standards, the Corvette was seen both as an image builder, while Chevrolet awaited its ohv V8, and as a serious sports car for the youth market. Its fibreglass body was certainly stylish and enabled the car to reach production quickly, but its 150 bhp

Above **Though the Vette was available only in white with a red interior, other Chevys now offered every colour of autumn and then some—no reversible hide, though**

Left **Two new magazines appeared in 1953, both in the popular school-book format. Petersen's** *Honk*, **however, changed its name to** *Car Craft* **in December**

'Stovebolt' straight-six engine wasn't going anywhere fast. The Corvette is still America's only real production sports car.

In the social world Ford celebrated their 50th birthday, while Lincoln romped home again with the first four places in the Carrera Panamericana, though keeping their present, the forthcoming Lincoln Continental, to themselves. Buick, on the other hand, invited us all to celebrate their golden anniversary with their first ohv V8, which produced 164 bhp

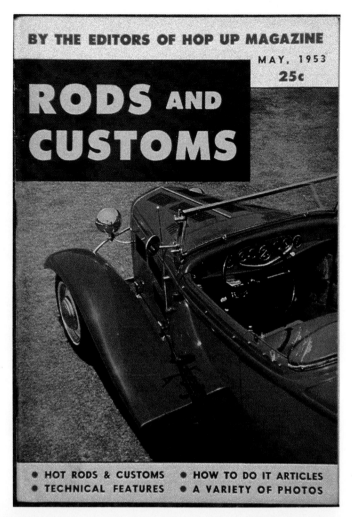

from its 322 cubic inches, and the Anniversary Convertible, otherwise known as the Skylark. Priced at a nice, round $5000, only 1690 were sold. Understandably, they are now very much in demand.

Until 1953 Studebaker had produced some very individual automobiles which, despite what looked like a hub cap stuck on the front, sold well enough. For 1953, in an effort to get out of the red, they introduced what was, in the words of *Motor Trend* magazine, 'The most refreshing, stimulating and progressively styled car'. Though credited to Raymond Loewy, what was conceived as a one-off special but became the Studebaker Champion was actually the work of Bob Bourke, an employee in Loewy's South Bend studio. Sadly, there were production problems and the car failed to get Studebaker's books into the black. It did, however, get into the record books, Bonneville racers loving its clean, slippery styling. Unfortunately, its uncluttered lines had almost no influence on the rest of the industry who went out on a wing for the next few years.

Above Motor Trend **magazine described the all-new 1953 Studebaker as 'The most refreshing, stimulating and progressively styled car to emerge from a stock car manufacturer since the days of the Lincoln Continental and the coffin-nosed Cord'. They were right; the rodders, if few other buyers, recognized this and have saved the Stude from extinction**

Top left Rods and Customs **eventually became just** *Rod & Custom*, **whereas** *Honk* **became** *Car Craft* **which is still Petersen Publishing's second string to** *Hot Rod* **magazine**

Bottom left **For 1953 Ford offered yet another restyled grille, an aeroplane hood ornament and a 50th anniversary crest for the centre of the steering wheel**

This was inexplicable if what was happening on the street was anything to go by. Customizers were going to great lengths to recreate the Champion's clean lines on other Detroit products. The car of the season was Jack Stewart's Polynesian, a radically restyled 1950 Olds 88. It actually looked a lot like Studebaker's Starlight coupé, being a tapered two-door hardtop shaved of all unnecessary chrome

and fitted with a wide, narrow grille. What really made it look long and low like the Stude was the removal of four inches from the sides of the car. This incredibly difficult operation was called sectioning and was, with the roof chop (though infinitely more complicated), the epitome of the customizers' art.

The art gained two new galleries that year when both *Hot Rod* and *Hop Up* launched two new magazines, *Rod & Custom* and *Honk* which, in December 1953, was renamed *Car Craft*.

In Russia, Joseph Stalin died, his secret policeman Lavrenti Beria was executed, and Nikita Khrushchev became First Secretary of the Communist Party. In England, Queen Elizabeth II was crowned and, to celebrate, Hillary and Tenzing nipped up Everest. We were also introduced to

Above **The first issue of** *Playboy* **was prepared on Hugh Hefner's kitchen table and with Marilyn Monroe naked over the centre pages was a recipe for success. Courtesy of Playboy Magazine: Copyright © 1953 by Playboy**

Left **Wurlitzer one for the money, two for the show and three to get ready—the King is coming**

James Bond, Ian Fleming's agent 007, William Burroughs' *Junkie*, and Hugh Hefner, who pioneered table-top publishing by producing the first issue of *Playboy* on his kitchen table. A naked centrefold of Marilyn Monroe might have had something to do with the first issue selling out. The Korean war ended, England won the Ashes and in Memphis, Tennessee, a kid called Elvis Presley walked into the Sun studios and asked Sam Phillips if he could record a song for his mother's birthday.

THE SHAPE OF FINS TO COME

By 1954 the Western world was getting into top gear, and while Roger Bannister ran a four-minute mile, the American public went on a spending spree. In England, where food rationing ended, they did much the same but there was really no comparison. The Americans were on course for somewhere totally alien to the rest of the world: the planet of plenty, a fantasy world of soaring skyscrapers, freeways and dream cars.

Almost every manufacturer had one, or more. Ford unveiled three: the FX Atmos, the Lincoln Monterey XK800, and the Mercury XM800, a fibreglass styling exercise on a stock chassis. Despite the impracticalities of innovations such as transparent plastic roofs, for the Mercury Monterey Sun Valley, which fried the occupants, Ford did manage to improve its market position. With the announcement of its long-awaited ohv V8 and its new two-seater Thunderbird it got within 9000 units of the number one sales spot, selling, along with Chevrolet, $1\frac{1}{2}$ million autos. Behind the scenes,

Left **Buick's Skylark Sport was basically a Century with grafted-on finned rear deck, no Ventiports but chrome wire wheels, leather trim and Easy-Eye glass**

Previous page **Ford went power crazy in 1954 with assisted seats, windows and brakes and a new 130 bhp ohv V8—25 per cent more powerful than the old side-valve flattie**

The Chevrolet Corvair

Here in this experimental two-passenger model with its glass fiber reinforced plastic body, Chevrolet brings new aerodynamic design to the closed sports car. The ultra-streamlined top sweeps back to a jet exhaust-type rear opening.

however, potentially disastrous decisions were being made, as a result of which poor Edsel's name would be ridiculed. Lincoln, despite another first and second in the Mexican road race, lost its fine mechanic Clay Smith, killed in a pit accident.

Buick were the trendsetters, though; their cars were lower, wider and, for the first time, sprouted stumpy, upswept, Cadillac-style ends to their rear wings—hardly the shape of fins to come, though. They also premiered the industry's first wraparound windscreen and revived the Buick Century, a smallish series 40 Special body fitted with the largish 322 ci Roadmaster engine. This factory hot rod was capable of 107 mph. Buick had its best year with sales approaching the three-quarter million mark.

After a glorious track record, poor old Hudson was having

Above **Though sold as the 'First of the dream cars to come true', sales of Chevy's Corvette were slow and variants like this Corvair coupé never made it to production**

Top left **The spinner hub cap, particularly those from the Dodge Lancer, either stolen or store bought, was America's most popular accessory; it still is for customizers**

Bottom left **If you couldn't afford the Cadillac, then at least you could afford these do-it-yourself, add-on Cad fins—no car should be without some**

a hard time. There was little money for development—a new Hornet Special failed to capture buyers as did the luxurious Jet-Liner. The latter, however, inspired Frank Spring to design a two-seater GT which was to be built in aluminium by Carrozzeria Touring of Milan. In all, 25 were built with 114 bhp engines, leather interiors, a wraparound screen,

your cars of tomo

the startling new Pontiac Strato Star

w are being designed at **Pontiac** today!

WORLD OF TOMORROW STYLING

fender scoops and doors cut into the roof. As attention-grabbing as it was, it and the other more mundane models failed to save Hudson from being swallowed by Nash.

With Hudson out of the race, Dodge decided to step in. They used the Firearrow show car, driven by Betty Skelton, to set the woman's world speed record at 143.44 mph; provided the official pace car for the Indy 500, a Royal convertible with chrome wire wheels and continental kit; introduced 'PowerFlite' transmission and added 10 bhp and the word Jet (Ram Jet) to the hemi engine. The latter enabled them to take the lead on the ovals, scoop the first four places in their class for the Panamericana and run more than 102 mph on a Californian dry lake.

Having come in from the lakes, the hot rodders were also on the move. In fact, for three years *Hot Rod* magazine and the NHRA toured the United States with the Safety Safari, helping to establish the sport. The gospel reached the East Coast late in 1954 when the first real Eastern drag race was held at the Linden airport in New Jersey. Their success was not matched by the French in the Far East, who surrendered to the Viet Minh.

Above **Ford's World of Tomorrow Styling consisted of show cars from each of the three divisions. The big news, however, was a new ohv V8 nicknamed the Y-block**

Top left **'54 Chevy Bel Air Sport coupé with more teeth than originally intended; wraparound parking lamps were new as was 'fashion fiesta' two-tone upholstery**

Bottom left **The Kaiser Darrin was another tibreglass sports roadster with unique doors which disappeared into the front wings. Sadly, only 435 were built**

Previous page **Pontiac's Strato Star show car gave some indication in the bumper and hood treatment of what was to come. Scalloped wings caught on with customizers**

Chrysler, however, succeeded in harnessing the gas-turbine engine but failed to put it into production for ten years. Of more immediate interest to the public were the four-barrel carb, dual exhausts and the spinner hub cap, which would be universally adopted as a badge of recognition by customizers. Chrysler advertised their wares as 'Anything less. . . Yesterday's Car!' What they failed to mention was that they were selling yesterday's styles; at least, they were trying to—sales actually fell by 40 per cent.

THE HOT ONE

Marlon Brando had been flexing the muscles of his Actor's Studio 'whole body acting' method in the 1954 films *On The Waterfront* and *The Wild One*, which was banned in England for more than 20 years, but in 1955 a new face would grip unsuspecting but eagerly awaiting cinema audiences.

The face, which was soft and vulnerable where Brando's was hard and defiant, belonged to James Dean, the rebel next door. His second film, *Rebel Without A Cause*, released just after his death in a newly acquired Porsche Spyder, froze him as a rebellious, car-crazy, alienated teenage son of middle-class parents. The famous 'chicken run' scene, in which Dean races the local gang leader towards the cliff edge, has him driving the classic kids' car, a Merc. Even if Dean was never to be confirmed by the passing of time as a great actor, his epitaph to live fast and die young conferred upon him anti-establishment hero status.

Dead or not, Dean personified youth who no longer had

Left **Ford challenged the Corvette with another European-flavoured sports car, the Thunderbird, and a new 292 ci Thunderbird V8—unlike the Vette it grew fat and ugly**

Previous page **Chevy changed the name of the game in '55 with the introduction of their 'Hot One', the 265 ci V8 which was, and still is, the American racing engine**

to listen to their elders and who at last had the purchasing power to do as they liked, but who needed one last ingredient to make their world perfect. That ingredient was music.

Billboard began publishing best-selling record charts in 1940, but in 1955 they introduced their first Top 100 chart and in 1958, as the Hot 100, this became the American industry standard.

The sound of rock and roll, a phrase coined by DJ Alan Freed, was first heard in the cinema where audiences were watching *The Blackboard Jungle* and hearing the title music 'Rock Around The Clock' by Bill Haley and his Comets. It immediately became the anthem of dissenting youth, staying at number one for 25 weeks. Bill, possibly realizing his fallibility, quickly released follow-ups and a poor film of the same title. Haley's problem was that, unlike Dean, he neither was nor looked young. What his flock needed was a preacher of their own age. The messiah was but a year away but his disciple, Chuck Berry, who got to number five in 1955 with 'Maybellene', was already amongst us.

Also fighting for the number one slot were Ford and Chevy, and both came to the battle with new designs. Chevy attacked on all fronts; at the bottom end of the market with a totally new low-priced line and up-market with the

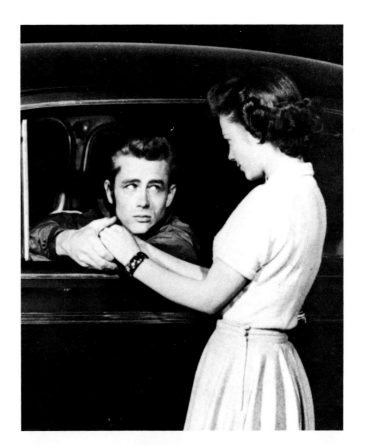

Left Chuck Berry, doing his famous duck-walk, more than any other songwriter, captured the affinity between sex and cars and rock 'n' roll. London Features International Ltd

Above right **James Dean—from** *East Of Eden* **to a** *Giant,* **but all the time a** *Rebel Without A Cause.*

Picture courtesy of the David Loehr Collection

*Right The Wild One—***Marlon Brando, unlike Dean, was never the vulnerable kid next door, nor was co-star Lee Marvin, who is still superbly playing the same part**

Corvette, both being aimed squarely at the young. The new saloon had smooth uncluttered lines, wraparound screens, Ferrari-style egg-crate grille, anti-dive front suspension, 12-volt electrics and a brand-new ohv V8 engine also used in the Corvette. This engine was light, strong and, with only 265 cubes, powerful at 162 bhp. It turned the Corvette into a real sports car, giving it a 0 to 60 mph time of just 8.7 seconds. It did the same for the saloons which, though the most popular cars in the US, had never enjoyed any kind of

Above **At the bottom of the Oldsmobile heap was the 88, but the high-horsepower Ninety-Eight Rocket V8 was an option to make the very desirable Super Eighty-Eight**

Top left **Not to be outdone, Dodge also restyled for '55 and came out more than six inches longer and with the title 'Flair-Fashion' and tri-colour paint**

Bottom left **And what were American teenagers doing at the time? Why, cruising to the new sound of rock 'n' roll—they were too young to drink but old enough to drive**

performance image. But suddenly here was a desirable and, what's more, affordable factory hot rod with plenty of potential. Chevy had a good year; they sold a record number of 1.7 million cars.

Ford fought back with a fleet of new Fairlanes, named after Henry Ford's mansion in Dearborn, and the Thunderbird, launched the previous September—but it was not enough to counter Chevrolet. Mercury also introduced a new range as it separated from Lincoln, but basically they were Fords.

Though the kids were still driving predominantly Ford-based street rods, the side-valve had faded in favour of ohv, and the car which set the trend for a decade or more was basically a 1923 Model T. It was built by budding actor

Norm Grabowski and was featured on the October 1955 cover of *Hot Rod*—it even appeared in *Life* magazine. It was powered by a '52 ohv Cadillac engine, and because of its outrageous open-wheel look was the forerunner of what became known as California fad-Ts or bucket-Ts. When it appeared on TV in the series *77 Sunset Strip* every kid in America wanted one, and quite a few started building

Above **Buick's face-lift for '55 included a new oval grille and new front and rear fenders, the latter housing 'tower' tail-lights. Scallops and pin-stripes were custom trends**
replicas.

Ohv engines were understandably making big noises at the racetrack. At the first NHRA Nationals, held in Great Bend, Kansas, the Bustelbomb, fitted with two engines, an

Olds in front and a Caddy in the back, reached 151 mph from a standing start in the quarter mile. A hot rod '27 T driven by Ak Miller and Doug Harrison also reached the finish, in seventh place overall, in the 1955 Panamericana.

Chrysler were enjoying a winning streak as well, the 1955 Grand National being won by Tim Flock driving a Chrysler 300. The 300 was part of designer Virgil Exner's 'Flight Sweep' '100 Million Dollar Look', which looked not unlike the '53 Studebaker. Nevertheless, with 300 bhp, hence the title, it recorded a two-way mile average of over 130 mph at Daytona. What most people failed to notice was the way the tail-light castings kicked up into small peaks.

There was nothing small about the peaks on the back of

Above **Pontiac got new bodies with 'Silver Streak' hood bands and its first ohv V8 for 1955; there was even a 'Power Pack' option boosting bhp to 200**

Top left **Pickup trucks suddenly became something more than just utilitarian transport and as usual the battle was between Ford's F100 and the Chevy shown here**

Bottom left **Brightly painted hot rods like this with chromed and open engines appeared all over America after Grabowski's fad-T featured in** *Hot Rod* **and** *Life* **magazines**

the new Cadillac Eldorado; suddenly, almost unnoticed, they had grown from small soft stumps to sharp-edged fins, Cadillac had started something that nobody would be able or seem to want to stop. Sales reached a new high as well.

GET YOUR KICKS ON ROUTE 66

Henry Ford may have given the Americans the means of mobility with his Model T but he did not give them roads. That was no problem in pre-war days, the T was a go-anywhere sturdy beast, and besides, there really wasn't anywhere to go. After the war, however, there was a housing shortage, and to accommodate the booming population a lot of middle-class Americans moved out to what they called the suburbs. One such, designed by Abraham Levitt for a Long Island potato patch, housed 100,000 people. He rapidly moved on to other patches and the people followed in their automobiles. They were able to do so because Ike had authorized the 1956 Federal Highway Act generating

41,000 miles of interstate roads, the construction of which lined forever the face of America.

It was the old pigeon-and-seed syndrome: the more roads they built, the more cars they got. Suddenly the ad men were advocating that two was better than one and that two cars weren't a luxury, they were a necessity. A second car was

Left **At Ike's instigation the Americans embarked on a massive interstate road-building programme and all of a sudden Americans got busy going somewhere**

Previous page **1955 had been Buick's best year, but the rot set in as quality slipped. Their slogan 'when better automobiles are built Buick will build them' wasn't true**

THE IMPALA

You're invited to compare your personal concept of a dream car with the fabulous Impala — an experimental car representing the creative vision of Chevrolet and General Motors stylists and designers.

The Impala incorporates wholly new considerations in fine passenger car design from the standpoint of sleekness, safety and luxury. Magic and majesty have been lifted from the drawing board and blended with motoring adventure, pleasure and safety by Chevrolet and General Motors designers and engineers in every aspect and detail.

Low and graceful in appearance—powered by a 225-horsepower V8 engine . . . abounding in comfort and convenience . . . interiorly appointed in tasteful elegance . . . . the Impala exceeds its antelope name-sake in fleetness and is truly a dream car worthy of your realistic appreciation and approval.

needed to take the kids to school, to collect the groceries, to get to the club, the lake, the beach, the drive-in.

The drive-in—drive-in car wash, drive-in cinema, drive-in restaurant—was the new 'don't walk, ride' America. Suddenly the car was important as an accessory; you were what you drove, it was your status symbol and the bigger the better.

And they were getting bigger, at least the fins, which seemed to be contagious from Cadillac, were. If your car didn't have them, you could buy a stick-on set for most models for around $35.

Harley Earl's aeroplane fetish was beginning to take off when, towards the end of the year, Cadillac previewed the Eldorado Brougham Coupe. Not only did it have higher and sharper fins but also quad lights and front and rear

Above **Chevrolet showed a simply styled car which belied the shape of things to come, owed a lot to the Corvette but would not appear, and a name, Impala, which would**

Bottom left **Well, a lot of people came to look but look was all they did; sales slumped. New features included rounded wheel wells, new tail-lights and forward-thrust grille**

projectiles, first introduced in 1942, the former with black rubber tips which made them look even more like breasts. In fact, they were nicknamed Dagmars after a rather voluptuous starlet of that name of the era.

Chrysler's 100 Million Dollar Look had suddenly sprouted some, but at least they were backing them up with more power. The 300B now had 354 ci, 355 optional bhp and to prove its worth averaged 139.9 mph at Daytona for the World Passenger Car Speed Record. The air speed record

1956 FORD

POLICE

Available with the new "Interce
and Lifeguard Design fea

or'' Y-8 Engine of 215 h.p.

res for greater safety

Preferred by

Law Enforcement Agencies

everywhere

was also increased that year, though not by Chrysler, to 1132 mph by a Fairey Delta fighter.

Chrysler's company Dodge, riding on a sales crest, left almost well alone except for increasing output to 260 bhp and introducing push-button gear selection and their own spinner hub cap for the Lancer. This was such a popular accessory most went missing as soon as it got dark.

Buicks had the makings of fins for their 1956 line-up; in fact, over there chrome was really catching on. There was a new, thrusting grille for all models and now four fake Ventiports for everything except the Special.

At Chevrolet Ed Cole was rewarded for his success with the General Manager's job, and to celebrate they too threw a little more glitter at the production line. They also added a beautiful two-door convertible Bel Air to the range and restyled the Corvette, shamelessly cribbing from the La Salle II show car and Mercedes' 300SL. The power output was increased from 195 to 225 and the 0 to 60 mph time fell to 7.3 seconds. Their merit prize was a championship win in the Sports Car Club of America C class.

Ford's so-called sports car was 50 bhp down on the Chevy and the relocation of the spare wheel to the 'continental' position adversely affected both the handling and steering. One wonders what film star Clark Gable's supercharged T-bird was like to drive. Ford were

Top left Not at all aptly named, the Fairey FD-2 fighter which in 1956 took the world air speed record to 1132 mph

Left The drive-in was suddenly the place to go, the food was cheap and convenient and, what is more, people could see what you were by what you drove

Previous page Ford used the '55 body with minor exterior alterations; the interior was restyled with seat belts

Above 'Hound Dog' Elvis Presley was the catalyst the kids had waited for. Like them, he was into cars, Cadillacs in particular, as this fanzine photo circa 1956 shows.

Photograph courtesy of the Estate of Elvis Presley

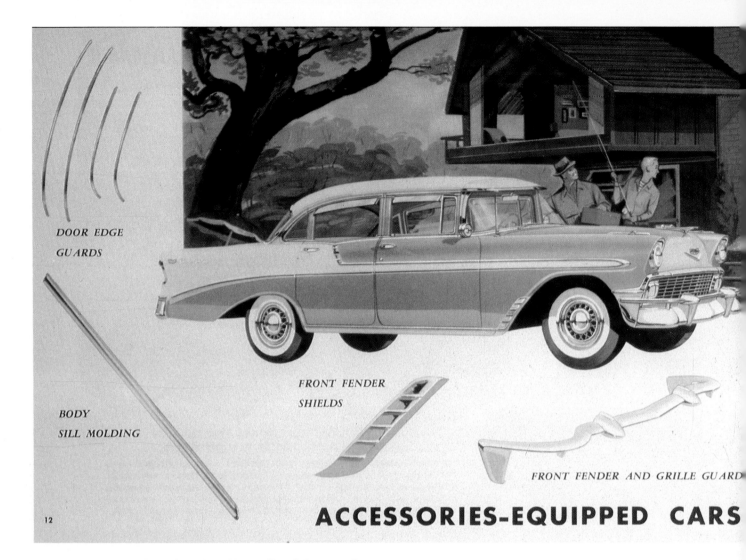

DOOR EDGE
GUARDS

BODY
SILL MOLDING

FRONT FENDER
SHIELDS

FRONT FENDER AND GRILLE GUARD

12

ACCESSORIES-EQUIPPED CARS

Above **For the more discerning driver Chevy offered the type of accessories which improved the quality of country club living—for the most part they glittered**

Previous page **The Hot Ones were, however, now available with an optional Super Turbo-Fire V8 producing 205 bhp, and Chevrolet instantly became king of the hill**

undoubtedly too busy floating their company—the Ford Foundation placed $10 million worth of shares on the market—to worry about their cars. They did find time, however, to release the long-awaited Lincoln Continental Mark II, which became an instant classic.

Mercury continued to go racing in 1956, winning five NASCAR Grand Nationals, and Bill Stroppe, driving JT450x

with a bored (to 391 ci) and injected Lincoln engine, ran 153 mph for the flying mile. Though hardly stock, it was a full-bodied factory car all the same; it was results such as this which would, in the near future, change the look of American racing. The quick car of the year, the Glass Slipper dragster, still used an sv Mercury and though it managed 181 mph at Bonneville, everybody could see that the engine was outdated.

The hot rodders were a tenacious bunch, though. One guy on his way to Daytona Speed Week had a wreck, rolled his coupé and crushed the roof. Rather than spoil his trip, he merely cut it off and raced his new roadster.

Pontiac until now had produced cars to make you yawn—

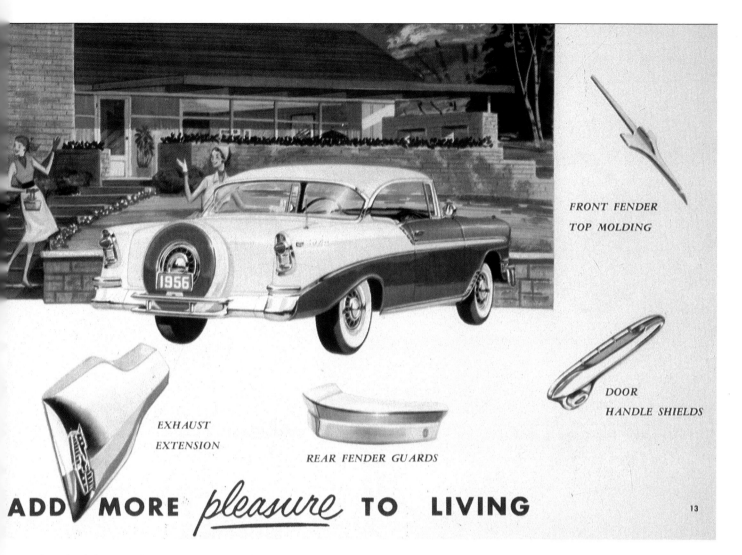

FRONT FENDER
TOP MOLDING

DOOR
HANDLE SHIELDS

EXHAUST
EXTENSION

REAR FENDER GUARDS

ADD MORE *pleasure* TO LIVING

13

they hadn't even had an ohv V8 until 1955. Now, with Bunkie Knudsen in charge and Pete Estes and a certain John Z. DeLorean heading the engineering group, they were going to change all that. At mid-year they announced so-called NASCAR, Super-Tempest and Super-Duty V8s. It would, however, be three years before the impact of this triumvirate was felt on the street. Packard, meanwhile, was swallowed by Studebaker.

Of course, the big noise that year was rock 'n' roll, which on occasion (it was by no means universally popular) could be heard belting out of Wurlitzers, Plymouth's Highway Hi-Fi record player and radios across the land. Chuck Berry's 'Roll Over Beethoven' made number one and stayed in the charts for 29 weeks, but his record was nothing compared to the King. Elvis' first release, 'Heartbreak Hotel', was charted for 22 weeks and number one for eight, while 'Don't Be Cruel' and 'Hound Dog' were there for 24 weeks and number one for 11. All together, he had 11 records in the charts that year and five of them went to number one.

The charts had been invaded, but then so had Hungary, by the Russians, Egypt by the French and the English, and the Sinai by the Israelis.

It was a busy year all right, but the future was secure: Ike was re-elected in November, Grace Kelly met and married her Prince, and a lot of people saw Brigitte Bardot's naked derrière at the cinema.

ON THE ROAD AND ALL SHOOK UP

No matter in which direction one looked, the world was no longer the place it had been. Too much was happening too fast—the human race was on. So was the space race when Russia successfully launched first Sputnik I and then II and the first Inter-Continental Ballistic Missile. The American attempt to launch an earth satellite failed.

The horsepower race was being run in Detroit where Chevrolet claimed that its fuel-injected 283 ci V8 Corvette engine was the first to produce one horsepower per cubic inch. Chrysler had made the same claim six months earlier for its 300B but Chevy shouted louder. They also revamped all their models again, the saloons gaining more front-end chrome, bomb sights and side-trim sweeping back into flat tail fins which hid the fuel filler. Lap belts and shoulder harnesses were new safety options listed alongside such life-saving devices as an accelerator pedal cover and the autronic eye. The following year they were replaced by two-tone paint.

Left **The Edsel's grille almost defies description and whatever one compares it to, nobody wanted to drive behind it. An estimated 300 million dollar miscalculation**

Previous page **Chevrolet, at the sharp end of the market, called the new range 'Sweet, Smooth and Sassy', but with 'Super Turbo-Fire 283' the hot rodders called it winner**

Low and Mighty for 1957

Chevy advertised the new models as 'The Hot One's Even Hotter' and 'Chevy Comes to the Line Loaded'; consequently, all three Chevys from '55 to '57 became instantly and extremely popular because of their simple style and performance potential.

The same criteria hold true today. Hot rodders and customers are still modifying Earl's masterpieces in any number of styles from low-and-slow boulevard cruisers to stripped-for-action racers.

Chevy's utility vehicles suddenly took on a new importance, which has remained constant ever since, when George Barris kustomized a '56 stepside pickup. He was

WEST BUICK YET

forced to do something different when his shop burned down and destroyed 14 vehicles. The Kopper Kart kontained a TV, record player, telephone and, for some unexplained reason, a komplete set of barber tools!

Chevy outsold Ford once again, though this time by a mere 136 cars, but as far as most people were concerned

GM's Buick also boasted revised styling for 1957 and a boost to 300 bhp. Four flattened Ventiports and Sweapspear moulding with chevrons were not enough to stop the slide

Ford took a disastrous turn in 1957. Their run-of-the-mill cars were restyled and reminiscent of the '56 Chevy, being both longer and lower (14-inch wheels were now standard)

America's Number 1 Ro

Above **Ford got their Thunderbird back on the right track for '57 by improving the handling and offering a 312 ci, 340 horsepower, Paxton supercharged V8**

Top left **Pontiac went to great lengths to acclaim the 'Star Flight' styling of its fuel-injected Star Chief Custom Bonneville with missile-shaped side-trim**

Bottom left **Under Harley Earl's direction GM products became bigger and bolder than ever, especially Cadillac's Eldorado Biarritz convertible with shark fins**

d Car . . .

than the previous models. Like all other cars that year, they sported tail fins, in Fordese, 'high-canted fenders'. It was a nice clean, if unexciting, car made interesting when they announced the Skyliner, the only true hardtop convertible in the world. Originally designed for the Lincoln, the roof mechanism, powered by three drive motors, four locking motors, ten power relays, eight circuit-breakers, ten cut-off switches and over 600 ft of wiring, was activated by one switch and never failed to impress.

The T-bird was similarly restyled and the spare was thrown back where it belonged. To enhance its image, Ford

made available a 340 bhp supercharged NASCAR V8.

That was the good news—the bad news was the Edsel. Many would say that the Edsel was announced just at the wrong time, there being a slight recession and a glut of big cars. But all the other big chrome boats were selling. What killed the Edsel was the grille. Neither men nor women seemed to mind driving phallic symbols but nobody was going to drive something which reminded them of a woman's vulva. The Edsel bombed in a big way, costing Ford hundreds of millions of dollars.

Despite larger fins, Virgil Exner's 'Forward Look' '57

SEPTEMBER 1957   25c

custom cars

How-to-do-it:
TWIN HOOD SCOOPS FOR '57 CHEVS

'50 MERC CHOPPED HARDTOP see page 34

Nerf Bar Craze

'Round Rod Restyling

Modernized Monterey

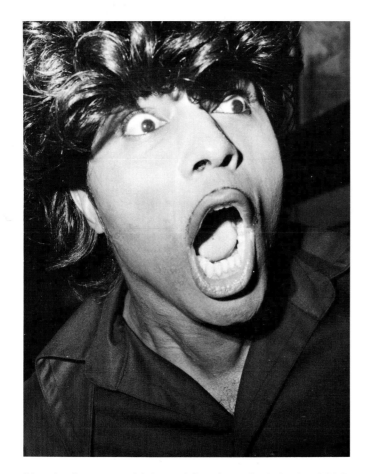 

Chrysler line was widely acclaimed, particularly the 300C two-door hardtop. It may have been big but it was clean, and the hemi now boasted 392 cubic inches, 375 bhp and, for the first time, Torsion-Aire suspension.

Not that Chrysler's Fire Power needed confirmation, but *Hot Rod* magazine took Plymouth's sister Savoy, dropped in a 389 ci Chrysler and clocked an official average of 159 mph. All that was about to end, though, when factory-backed racing was banned by the Automobile Manufacturers Association.

A factory racing ban did not, however, affect the drag racers, and that year Ken Lindley disproved the sceptics' theory that a dragster could not accelerate from a standing start to 150 mph in a quarter of a mile. His supercharged Chrysler-powered dragster went 159.01. At the other end of the scale the Go Kart was invented.

Above **'The Killer' Jerry Lee Lewis, one of rock's most dynamic performers, here minus 'His Pumping Piano', had a hit with his 'Great Balls Of Fire'**

Above left **Little Richard, often billed as 'The King of Rock 'n' Roll' after a film entitled** *Mr Rock 'n' Roll,* **had hits in '57 with 'Lucille', 'Jenny Jenny' and 'Keep A Knockin''**

Left **Another new magazine, this one aimed directly at customizers rather than hot rodders, appeared on the book stalls late in the year**

Previous page **Chrysler's DeSoto Firedome. The similar Adventurer was the first base model to offer one horsepower per cubic inch; Chevy's offering was optional**

Just as chrome had taken over the car, so rock 'n' roll took over the radio. Elvis had nine hits and released his first film, *Jailhouse Rock*. But he was no longer alone; Chuck Berry had hits with 'School Day' and 'Rock And Roll Music', Little

from steel hardtop...

At first glance you'd take the Skyliner for a new and distinctively different Victoria—a handsome all-weather car—as snug and safe as a steel hardtop can be, and the Skyliner is all of that! But what *hardtop* ever had a control on the instrument panel marked "Top"?

automatically

Touch the magic control and synchronized electric motors quietly go to work. Locking screws that secure the roof to windshield and body untwist . . . automatically! The roof swings back, vanishes smoothly out of sight into the rear deck. The deck lid closes—flush—and locks itself tightly in place.

...to open convertib

Now you're sitting pretty for sun and fun, Ford convertible
But should the clouds threaten, just touch the magic control ;
In less than a minute the roof is back in place and locked so
let you laugh at the worst of wind and weather.

Richard had three chart successes and a film called *Mr Rock 'n' Roll*. A newcomer, Jerry Lee Lewis, also got into the Hot 100 with 'Great Balls Of Fire' and 'Whole Lotta Shakin' Goin' On'. Towards the end of the year they all took a step towards the wings as out into the footlights stepped a bespectacled kid from Lubbock, Texas, named Buddy Holly, singing a song called 'Peggy Sue'. The chart-topper that year, however, was mushy 'Love Letters In The Sand' by Pat Boone, number one for 24 weeks.

Loving it all was author Jack Kerouac who declared, 'It is essential to dig the most for if you do not dig you lose your superiority over the square and so you are less likely to be cool'. Kerouac's book *On The Road* was the inspiration for

Above **Chevy, adding bomb sights to the hood, advertised their 1957 line as 'The Hot One's Even Hotter', the Corvette having optional fuel injection**

Left **Ford restyled for '57 making them longer and lower with rear opening hoods, streamlined wheel openings and 'high-canted fenders'**

Previous page **Ford's most dramatic offering was the Skyliner, the world's only true hardtop convertible. You were not advised to activate when mobile**

America, who took to Ike's interstates by the car-load, looking for the land promised by ad men. Wherever it was, it was certainly not Christmas Island where the British tested an H-Bomb. Nice present, that.

AT THE HOP

Fear that England itself might be the next test site galvanized a group of people into the Campaign for Nuclear Disarmament. They marched back and forth across the country and nobody in power took any notice.

Maybe Elvis, who was called up and shipped to Germany, would save the world. Despite national service he managed eight hits and another film, *King Creole*. The big chart success that year, though, was 'At The Hop' by Danny and the Juniors, which summarized the excitement coursing through American teenage life. Cruising Main Street on the weekend, drinking root beer at an A & W or eating popcorn at the drive-in; it was *West Side Story* and for them the cold

war was conducted on the back seat of a convertible. And what better than the all-new '58 Chevy.

It was Chevy's 50th birthday and the theme for the year was 'Forward from Fifty'. To mark the occasion they had a complete redesign, and with performance de-emphasized, as a result of the racing ban, everything was lower, wider and

Left **All dressed up and nowhere to go. The Cadillac Fleetwood limousine with shark fins. A 335 bhp Eldorado engine with three two-barrel carbs was optional**

Previous page **What better car to cruise than Chevy's new Impala. It was 'The Hot One' gone cold as Chevy stressed its 'Sculpturamic' styling rather than performance**

PROTECTION OPTIONS....

LOCKING GASOLINE CAP

DELUXE CONTOUR FLOOR MATS

RUBBER FLOOR MATS

POWER BRAKE

BACK UP LAMPS

ACCELERATOR PEDAL COVER

COURTESY LAMPS

AUTRONIC EYE

SEAT BELT   SHOULDER HARNESS

PARKING BRAKE SIGNAL

JUNCTION BLOCK

nine inches longer. They were cruisers from their quad lamps to their gull-wings, with plenty of chrome in between. Chevy promised 'the road-smoothingest, nerve-soothingest ride imaginable', and in so doing entered the boat race. The '58, apart from its nameplate, bore no comparison to its predecessors; nevertheless, it became 'the pre-eminent American car'.

Just about everybody had seen and copied Cadillac's chrome, fin and quad-light look, and though they no longer needed it for racing, copious amounts of horsepower were necessary to pull these cruisers from their berths and to power all the assisted accessories. The Eldorado Biarritz even had humidity sensors which automatically activated the top riser mechanism in the case of rain.

In order to cope, engine capacities continued to rise:

Above **The 'Truck for Tomorrow' was how** *Rod & Custom* **magazine described their reader-designed 'Dream Truck', based on an early-fifties Chevy pickup**

Top left **Safety was the big feature for '58 and Chevrolet offered seat belts which were so unpopular with the public that they were dropped the following year**

Bottom left **By the end of the decade the dragstrips, where the flathead had once ruled, were dominated by Chrysler's hemi. Picture courtesy of the Pat Ganahl Collection**

Chevy went to 348 ci, Cadillac 365, Buick 364, Chrysler 392, Ford 353, Mercury 383, and 370 for Pontiac. Seemingly they had not heard of the racing ban because late in the year they assembled some cars for NASCAR certification.

The industry had learned a new phrase, 'planned

THIS IS NO ORDINARY CAR

Brilliant new version of Ford's great American classic...the 4-passen

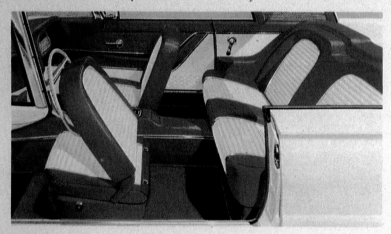

*Another First from Ford...a jewel of a car...
created to give more fun, more luxury
and full fine-car passenger room for four!*

Ford presents a wholly new size and new type of fine car. It gives you famed
Thunderbird distinction . . . Thunderbird compactness and maneuverability
. . . exciting Thunderbird performance—and *now* with full fine-car roomi-
ness, comfort and luxury for four! It's *twice the fun* to own a Thunderbird!

The 1958 Thunderbird seats four in full lap-of-luxury comfort

© 1957, Ford Motor Company, Dearborn, Mich.

**Above Ford flipped out for 1958 by totally destroying the
Thunderbird as a sports car concept. With four seats it became
just another big American boat**

Previous page **Nothing was ever more true than the advertising
copy for the Edsel, but they were wasting their time—nobody
wanted an extraordinary car**

obsolescence', and with this philosophy they intended to
ride out the decade. Who cared how crass the cars were
when the idea was to throw them away and get a new model
as soon as it was available. The last two years of the fifties
would see the car manufacturers go crazy decorating their
creations like Christmas-tree salesmen one minute before
midnight on Christmas Eve when there are no more buyers.

Ford fared no better than Chevy—in fact, they did worse.
At least Chevy had not ruined the Corvette. Ford, however,
waved a wand at the Thunderbird and turned Cinderella's
sports car into a white elephant. With four seats instead of
two, the Tudor hardtop coupé was now over 18 inches
longer and 1000 lb heavier than the previous model. Ford
was out of the American sports car race.

Lincoln also went too far in its attempt to outdo Cadillac.
The new Continental Mark III was, at almost six metres, the
largest passenger car on the market and had about as much
torsional strength as a piece of wet spaghetti. To pull it they
produced a 430 ci engine. They need not have bothered
because hardly anybody bought it; Lincoln were last but one

118

THUNDERBIRD

Now there's fun for <u>four</u> — in America's most individual car

in the small-ships sales race.

Chrome was catching, even the customizers who had been clean if not conservative in their automotive expression seemed suddenly to discover it. Perhaps it was just their developed desire to be different that caused them to go to extremes, but they too began to decorate their cars like Christmas trees. *Rod & Custom* magazine built, according to readers' suggestions, the 'Truck for Tomorrow' and adorned it with scallops and scoops, fins and four lamps, even a few Ventiports for full measure. While touring the country's car shows it was wrecked. Barris tried much the same treatment on a '29 Model A Ford pickup he called Ala Kart. With 30 coats of pearlescent paint, it twice won America's Most

Beautiful Roadster title but it too was destroyed. Was somebody trying to say something?

Now, maybe more than ever, it was a time for extremes. At the drags the Arfons brothers first tried Allison aircraft engines and, later, jet engines.

Seemingly the only people left building clean cars were the sports car racers. In particular, Lance Reventlow, heir-apparent to one of the world's largest fortunes, tried to build an American car to compete with the best that Europe fielded. His Chevy-powered Scarab was simply beautiful.

The irrevocable course for the following year had long been set by the production process but what nobody was sure of was whether the public would still come for the ride.

119

BISCAYNE
TWO-DOOR SEDAN

MORE AMERICANS HAVE MORE

As the decade came to a close, there was the stark realization that this was not the same world it had been ten years ago. Then, not one but two major conflicts had taken place, the world had survived and there was optimism for a better future. Suddenly the future was the present and it didn't look all that bright. There was insurrection in both the Southern states and in England where blacks fought for recognition. In Cuba, Fidel Castro ousted the Batista regime described by John F. Kennedy as 'one of the most bloody and repressive dictatorships in the long history of Latin America'—it had been American backed. They had lost a strategic base but more importantly to most Americans a holiday resort.

Thankfully they got two in return: Alaska, which wasn't worth visiting but had oil, and Hawaii which was.

It was not a time to be selling tomorrow's world today but Detroit had no choice, the cars were coming off the line. Buick brought out its wildest, with blade fins stretching the full 5½ metres of its length and a 401 ci engine. Chevrolet's

Left **Dodge used space-age inspiration to dramatic effect in its copious use of chrome and radical tail-light design; at least they backed it up with a 345 bhp Super D500 V8**

Previous page **Buick, Chevrolet and Cadillac all battled for the biggest and best fins. Chevy won with the widest as they grew to the full width of the car**

123

An exciting new **EXPERIMENTAL**

Chevrolet Corvette...

restyled Impala had full-width fins, a full complement of chrome and 'Special Super Turbo-Thrust V8'. Dodge merely exaggerated everything with what they called 'Swept-Wing Styling' for a longer, lower, wider car with longer and higher fins and raised eyebrows which were not only on the headlights. Plymouth renamed their range and canted their fins, while Pontiac, not content with two, split their fins into four. Cadillac, who started all this, at least had the dignity to see it out in style for theirs were the biggest and undoubtedly best of all. Two massive fins would suffice but they were adorned with twin rocket-motor tail-lights. The only way out now was down.

Strange that the progenitor of this extravagance, Harley Earl, should build and keep for his personal use after retirement a Ferrari-style, Oldsmobile-based roadster which had little of the flamboyant styling he had been famous for. Perhaps it was all a bad-taste joke.

Some had already seen the way, evangelist Billy Graham

Above **Plymouth replied with their 'double-barrel' front fender 'Forward Look' and new Sport Fury line. An optional engine was the 360 ci 305 bhp 'Golden Commando'**

Top left **The front end of the new Dodge raised a few eyebrows, especially over the headlights. The new cars were longer, lower and wider, as were everybody's**

Bottom left **Chevrolet thankfully never lost direction with its Corvette, and Zora Arkus Duntov opened the new Daytona Speedway in this experimental SS**

for one, also Ford, Lincoln and Mercury whose fins almost disappeared in 1959. It was the company's first sensible move for some years.

There were many who lamented the end of this era but it was inevitable, new things had to be tried. Chevrolet saw the way with the rear-engined, air-cooled, flat-six Corvair introduced in October 1959. Compared with all other American cars it was unconventional and uncluttered. *Motor Trend* magazine proclaimed it 'Car of the Year'; public

saviour number one Ralph Nader proclaimed it 'Unsafe at Any Speed'.

At least the Corvette had not lost its direction—it was still a sports car, as the men behind it proved when they took a special magnesium-bodied SS version to Daytona and turned lap speeds in excess of 150 mph.

Ford also introduced a new compact car in October 1959. Called the Falcon, it was conservative and conventional and, unlike the Corvair, would enjoy an illustrious career both on and off the track.

At the track everybody was talking about a Florida-based racer who had appeared on the scene. His name was Don Garlits, he raced a black Chrysler-powered dragster, and he turned constant quarter miles in under nine seconds with speeds above 170 mph. He is still one of the world's fastest men on four wheels. The air speed record was also increased that year to 1520 mph.

In the record charts things were also different, the hard

Above **Buick won the battle for the longest because their blade fins ran the full length, 5.5 metres, of the car, which could be had with a 401 ci engine**

Previous page **Cadillac won the tall-ships race with their towering shark fins which were further enhanced by twin bullet tail-lights—it was the end of the line for fins and the fifties**

edge of rock 'n' roll having been rounded off just like the fins of the cars would be. Chuck Berry went to jail, Jerry Lee Lewis was ostracized, Buddy Holly was killed in a plane crash, Alan Freed was implicated in a payola scandal, and Little Richard and Elvis the Pelvis had been replaced by the warbling sound of Bobby Darin, in the charts for 22 weeks with 'Mack The Knife'.

In England they opened the M1, Britain's first motorway, but was it to be the freeway to Utopia it had been in America? Prime Minister Harold Macmillan declared 'You've never had it so good!', but Britain had just never had it.